★

THE ALAMO

★ 300 YEARS OF TEXAS HISTORY ★

OFFICIAL COMMEMORATIVE GUIDE

BECKON BOOKS

Alamo Church
This haunting depiction of the Alamo church was painted by Verner White in the 1880s and shows the two-story Hugo & Schmeltzer Company store atop the Long Barrack.

Welcome to the Alamo

Most people remember the Alamo as a heroic struggle against impossible odds—a place where men made the ultimate sacrifice for freedom. The 1836 battle, however, is only one piece of the Alamo's long and storied past.

Founded as Mission San Antonio de Valero in 1718, the Alamo played a crucial role in the Spanish settlement of Texas and became a focal point for 300 years of historic change in the American Southwest. The small stone mission was one of Spain's first along the Texas frontier. The Alamo's significance as a Spanish mission quickly made it—and the town that sprung up around it—the cultural and commercial center of the region. Consequently, when the Texas Revolution began in 1835, San Antonio became strategically important to both Mexican and Texian forces.

The Alamo also played an important part in the formation of America and impacted world history. The Texian defeat at the Alamo led to the ultimate victory over Mexican general Antonio López de Santa Anna at San Jacinto and Texas independence. The ongoing fight over the Republic of Texas led to annexation by the United States and sparked war with Mexico in 1846. The American victory in that war expanded the frontier to the Pacific Ocean in fulfillment of Manifest Destiny and gave the United States vast new territories full of wealth and promise. And the gold, cattle, oil, and cotton that flowed from these territories fueled the nation and contributed to its role as a world power after the turn of the 20th century.

During your visit, it's important to remember both the 1836 battle and the Alamo's rich and complex past. In doing so, you'll gain a better understanding of one of America's most significant places, the cradle of Texas liberty.

Coahuiltecan Indians

The lowlands of northeastern Mexico and southern Texas were originally occupied by hundreds of Indian groups that lived by hunting and gathering. Collectively called the Coahuiltecan people, they spoke numerous languages and dialects. In the 1700s, the Spanish initiated contact with the Coahuiltecans and established missions throughout the region. While successful, the cultural transformation included negative aspects such as greatly harming the native population through disease and disrupting their traditional way of life. About 1,200 of these indigenous people lived in the missions of San Antonio, including Mission San Antonio de Valero. After the missions were secularized in the late 1700s, the remaining Coahuiltecan communities were absorbed into the Hispanic culture.

The Mission Period

1700 - 1793

The Alamo's story begins in 1700 with the establishment of the Mission San Francisco de Solano near the Rio Grande in Coahuila, Mexico. There, Father Antonio de San Buenaventura y Olivares sought to convert the indigenous Coahuiltecan people to Catholicism, the official religion of Spain. In 1709, Olivares traveled to Texas and was struck by the potential of the San Antonio area for a new mission. He recommended it to the Spanish viceroy, Marqués de Valero, as a waypoint for travelers going east. In 1718, with Valero's approval, Olivares relocated Mission San Francisco Solano and renamed it San Antonio de Valero in honor of Saint Anthony de Padua and the viceroy.

The mission's purpose was to convert the Coahuiltecan people to Catholicism and the Spanish way of life. In doing this, the Spanish hoped to create a self-sufficient population of loyal Spanish subjects and fend off any involvement from foreign powers like France.

For 75 years, San Antonio de Valero was home to Spanish missionaries and their Indian converts. The Coahuiltecans raised livestock and were taught farming, blacksmithing, carpentry, stonework, and weaving. In addition to food and shelter, the mission provided protection to the indigenous people in the form of firearms and horses.

By the late 1700s, the number of Indian converts had dwindled at most of the Spanish missions, and the rich lands were coveted by many local populations. In 1793, Mission San Antonio de Valero was secularized and control passed to local authorities. The former mission, with its convent, adobe houses, and incomplete stone church, would have an even greater legacy as a military garrison.

Map of New Spain
This map from 1720 entitled "Kingdom of Mexico, or New Spain, Louisiana, New England, Carolina, Virginia and Pennsylvania" shows Texas just as the Spanish were solidifying control over it and extinguishing the French threat to the territory shown in red.

Rosary with Cross
The tradition of the rosary dates to the 13th century and was an important part of daily Catholic devotion at the Spanish missions.

"On the 5th of May, the governor [Alarcón], in the name of his Majesty, took possession of the place called San Antonio.... This site is henceforth destined for the civil settlement and the soldiers who are to guard it, as well as for the site of the mission of San Antonio de Valero."

—Diary of Fray Francisco Céliz, Alarcón Expedition to settle San Antonio de Béxar, May 5, 1718

Marqués de Valero
Mission San Antonio de Valero (the Alamo) was named in part for Don Baltasar de Zúñiga, the second Marqués de Valero. Viceroy Zúñiga approved the establishment of the Spanish missions in Texas.

DON BALTASAR D. ZVÑIGA
MARQUES D VALERO
NACIO EN BEJAR EN 1659
MVRIO EN MADRID EN 1727
FVÉ VIRREY D MÉXICO
Y FVNDO EN TEXAS LA
CIVDAD D SAN ANTONIO

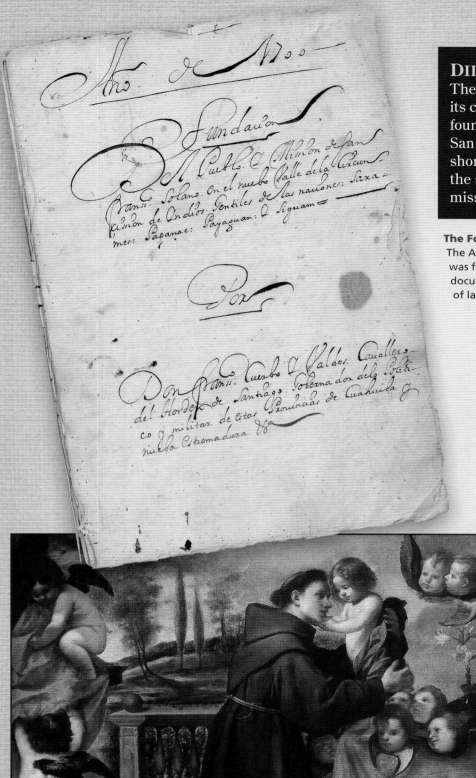

DID YOU KNOW?

The Mission Valero has not always been at its current site. The original mission was founded in 1718 near the headwaters of the San Pedro Creek. A year later, it was moved a short distance away. After a storm destroyed the site in 1724, Spanish officials moved the mission to its present and final spot.

The Founding of Mission San Francisco Solano
The Alamo's predecessor, Mission San Francisco Solano, was founded on March 1, 1700, near the Rio Grande. This document, the Act of Possession, signified the transfer of land from the Crown to the missionaries.

Statue of Saint Anthony
Mission San Antonio de Valero was named in part for Saint Anthony de Padua. San Antonio is the largest city to be named for the saint. This statue is dated 1730.

Saint Anthony
This 17th century painting is Antonio de Pereda's *Saint Anthony of Padua with Christ Child*. A Franciscan friar and powerful orator, Saint Anthony was canonized just one year after his death in 1231.

"*For the greater glory of God and of his Blessed Mother, on this site and spot I established this town and mission, and gave it the name of San Francisco Solano.*"

—A portion of the Act of Possession, performed by Sargento Mayor Diego Ramón and Father Antonio de Olivares for Mission San Francisco Solano, the predecessor of Mission San Antonio de Valero

Decline of Spanish Rule

1794 - 1821

At the turn of the 19th century, Spain mobilized its military along the Texas frontier in response to threats from France and the United States. The Spanish military occupied the old mission compound of San Antonio de Valero. Soon, it was converted into a frontier outpost and military garrison.

The first soldiers to arrive were part of La Segunda Compañía Volante de San Carlos de Parras, the Second Flying Company of San Carlos de Parras. Also called the Alamo Company, the soldiers were named for their hometown of Alamo de Parras, located south of the Rio Grande. One hundred soldiers and their families arrived in 1803. The mission's old *convento* (convent) became a barrack, and the second story became a military hospital—the first hospital in Texas. Soon, people were calling the old mission the Pueblo de la Compañía del Alamo, eventually shortening it to "the Alamo." The troops protected the San Antonio area from Indian raiders; escorted travelers, merchants, and officials around the region; and intercepted encroaching Americans. Momentous events, however, tested their loyalty.

Father Miguel Hidalgo
Miguel Hidalgo, a Mexican priest, is known as the father of Mexican independence. He launched a revolt against Spain in 1810 but was martyred soon after.

DID YOU KNOW?
During the fight for Mexican independence in 1811, Spanish governor Manuel Salcedo arrested two Alamo soldiers for fostering revolt. Salcedo then ordered the Alamo garrison to leave for an attack against the Mexican rebels. In response, a coalition of locals and soldiers threw their support to Mexican captain Juan Bautista de las Casas. Casas arrested Governor Salcedo and briefly imprisoned him in the Alamo jail.

In 1810, Father Miguel Hidalgo launched an anti-Spanish revolt that spread across Mexico and extended into Texas. Although the soldiers were supposed to battle the rebels, some members of the Alamo Company joined the Mexican revolutionaries and American volunteers who were attempting to transform Texas into an independent republic. One of the bloodiest battles occurred in August 1813 when a Spanish Royalist army crushed an independence movement at the Battle of Medina. Afterward, the company resumed its traditional role, but American filibusters continued to threaten Texas.

Spanish Dirk
This Spanish dirk, or dagger, dates from the 18th century and is representative of the Spanish colonial weaponry used during the period.

"The Mexican Nation, which for three hundred years has neither had its own will, nor free use of its voice, leaves today the oppression in which it has lived."

—Mexican Declaration of Independence from Spain, September 28, 1821

José Francisco Ruiz

Colonel José Francisco Ruiz was born in 1783 in San Antonio de Béxar, Mexico (later Texas). He was the first schoolteacher in San Antonio de Béxar as well as a town councilor and city attorney. He spent most of his career, however, in the military. In 1813, Ruiz fought with the Republican army in the Battle of Medina. After the army's defeat, he fled to Louisiana and traded with the Comanches. He returned when Mexico gained independence in 1822 and was assigned to assess parts of Texas. Ruiz joined the Texas Revolution and was one of the two Tejanos to sign the Texas Declaration of Independence. Under the republic, he became the first senator from the San Antonio de Béxar district. Ruiz died in 1840.

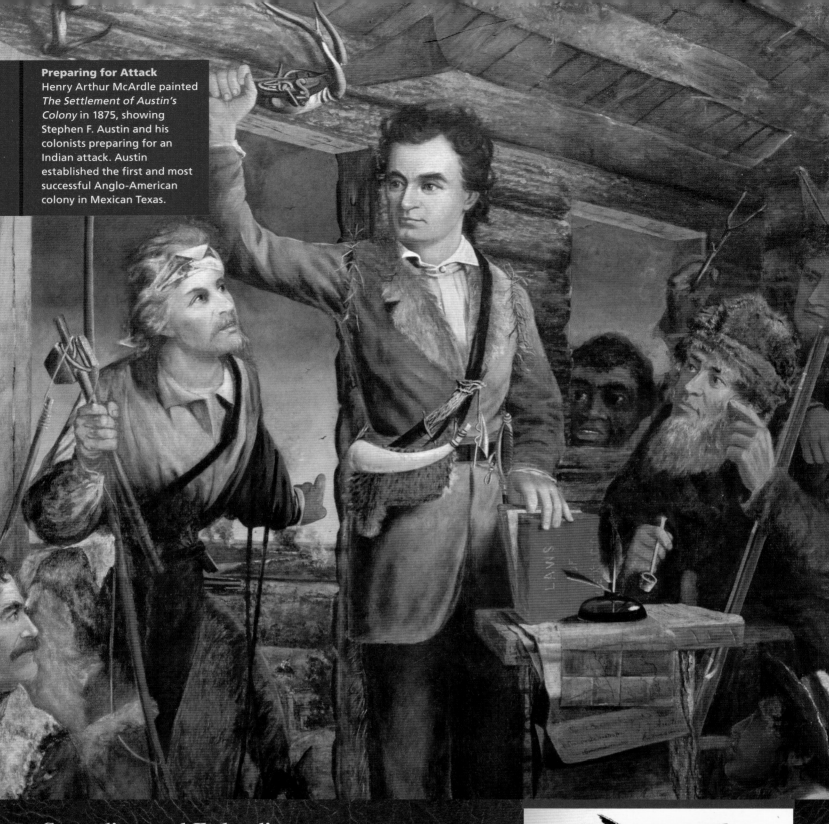

Preparing for Attack
Henry Arthur McArdle painted *The Settlement of Austin's Colony* in 1875, showing Stephen F. Austin and his colonists preparing for an Indian attack. Austin established the first and most successful Anglo-American colony in Mexican Texas.

Centralists and Federalists

The creation of the Federal Republic of Mexico in 1821 enabled upward movement for the developing class of professionals—called Federalists or Republicans. This threatened the traditional authority of the older class of Mexican Centralists, a powerful political party that included the national army, the Catholic Church, and large landowners. The Centralists favored consolidating government control from central Mexico, while the Federalists supported the democratic Federal Constitution of 1824. This political-societal conflict would lead to decades of civil war as rival political factions struggled to control Mexico and its holdings. The Texas Revolution was one of several uprisings against the Centralist government. At right is the symbol of Mexican federalism, taken from the 1828 Constitution for the State of Coahuila y Tejas.

Grabado de la "Colección de Constituciones de los Estados Unidos Mexicanos", en la cual fue publicada por primera vez en 1828 la Constitución del Estado de Coahuila y Texas.

Mexican Texas

The Alamo's soldiers shifted their allegiance to the Republic of Mexico when the newly formed country declared independence from Spain in 1821. Yet like Spain, Mexico had trouble holding and governing Texas. The region had just three sparsely populated communities: Nacogdoches, Presidio La Bahía (Goliad), and San Antonio de Béxar. To bolster Texas's dwindling population, the Mexican government began encouraging immigration from the United States in 1823. The government granted contracts to land agents called *empresarios* who would ensure that law-abiding men and women settled in Texas. Within five years, the immigrant population grew from about 500 to more than 30,000.

In 1824, Mexico adopted a constitution that established a federal-style government. The new nation was divided into 18 states, each with its own governor and legislature. Because it lacked sufficient inhabitants, Texas was designated the Department of Texas and placed within the state of Coahuila y Tejas. Native-born Texans (Tejanos) felt slighted. They called for separate statehood, banding together with incoming settlers to support colonization.

On April 6, 1830, the Mexican government prohibited the settlement of emigrants from the United States in an effort to stem the tide of immigration. Three years later, Antonio López de Santa Anna was elected president, obtaining extralegal powers to combat growing Federalist opposition in states like Coahuila y Tejas. He became absolute ruler of Mexico.

Meanwhile, in San Antonio de Béxar, the Alamo Company was ordered to retrieve a small cannon loaned by the Mexican government to the nearby town of Gonzales for protection against Indian raids. Commanded by Francisco Castañeda, the soldiers encountered resistance from the colonists, who taunted, "Come and take it!" On October 2, 1835, they fired on Castañeda's men, igniting the Texas Revolution.

1824 Mexican Constitution
The Mexican Constitution of 1824 joined Texas with Coahuila to make a single state with its governor headquartered in the capital of Saltillo.

Petition to Settle 300 Families in Texas
On December 26, 1820, Moses Austin of Missouri petitioned the Mexican governor of Texas to settle 300 families in Texas. His petition was approved in this January 17, 1821, letter from the provincial deputation in Monterey to the town council in San Antonio.

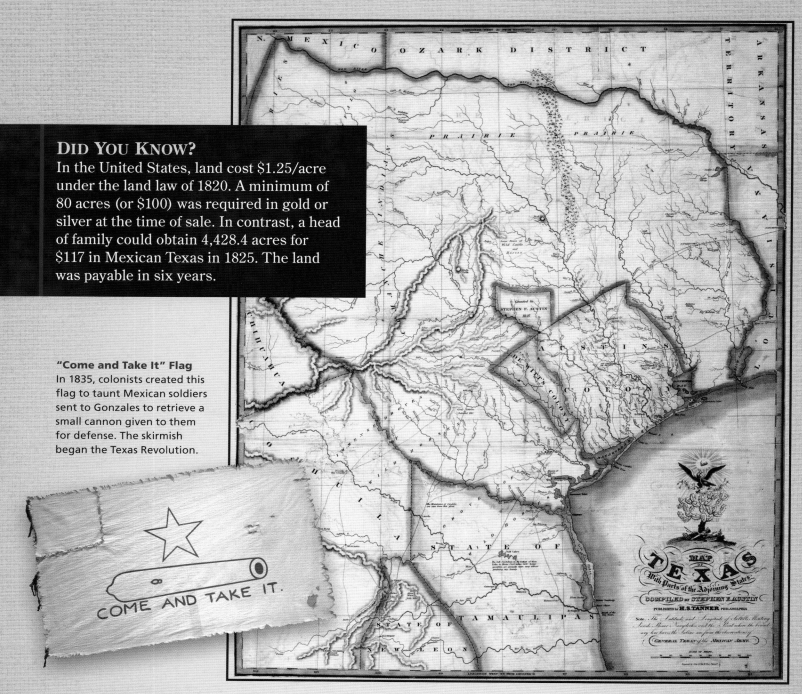

"Come and Take It" Flag
In 1835, colonists created this flag to taunt Mexican soldiers sent to Gonzales to retrieve a small cannon given to them for defense. The skirmish began the Texas Revolution.

Stephen F. Austin's Map of Texas
When Stephen F. Austin took over his father's Texas colonization plans in 1821, he promised Mexican authorities he would compile an accurate map of Texas. This 1830 map is the result.

"The die is cast, and something will be done in a few months towards effecting a separation of Texas, from the Mexican Republic. I have military honors . . . and receive a pension from the government of Mexico. I will lose it all rather than go to Mexico and unite myself to the ranks of that oppressive army."

—José Francisco Ruiz to his nephew José Antonio Navarro, March 1835

Veramendi Doors

Juan Martín de Veramendi was born in San Antonio and became a prominent local merchant, leader, and governor of Coahuila y Tejas. His daughter Ursula was married to Alamo defender James Bowie. These doors from the Veramendi home are on display at the Alamo.

Stephen F. Austin

Stephen F. Austin was born in 1793. His father, Moses Austin, was one of the first people to plan large-scale Anglo colonization of Texas. When his father died in 1820, Stephen Austin carried on the work. Austin became the first *empresario* of Texas, drawing up criminal and civil codes, instituting an appellate court, working to maintain harmony with the Mexican government, and maintaining the complicated land system. By 1832, his colonies comprised 8,000 people. In 1835, Austin joined the Texas Revolution and led the rebels during the Siege of Béxar. He served as commissioner for the provisional government and secretary of state under the republic. He died in 1836. Today, the state capital is named in his honor.

Texas Revolution

San Antonio de Béxar had long been an important place in Texas. Not only was it a military garrison, it was also a crossroads of culture and commerce. By the early 1830s, the town served as the capital of the region with a population of nearly 2,500.

San Antonio experienced two sieges during the Texas Revolution. The first was the Siege of Béxar, which began in late October 1835 when angry rebels followed the retreating Alamo Company back to San Antonio from Gonzales. When the attempt to take the town stalled, soldier and *empresario* Benjamin Milam rallied an attack on December 5. After a bloody, five-day, house-to-house fight, Mexican general Martín Perfecto de Cos surrendered San Antonio and the Alamo.

The second siege occurred on February 23, 1836, when General Antonio López de Santa Anna and his army arrived at San Antonio to put down the rebellion. The rebels withdrew into the safety of the Alamo and engaged in a protracted battle. It culminated in a 90-minute, famous last stand in which the defenders were overwhelmed.

On March 2, while the Alamo was under siege, the provisional Texas government meeting at Washington-on-the-Brazos declared independence. After the battle ended, Santa Anna pursued the Texian troops eastward and ordered the massacre of Texians captured near the Goliad mission. When he approached present-day Houston, Santa Anna split his forces and backed himself into a corner along Buffalo Bayou. On April 21, Texian general Sam Houston launched a surprise attack on Santa Anna. He defeated the larger Mexican army in only 18 minutes, capturing Santa Anna and achieving independence.

The Treaty of Velasco was signed on May 14, 1836, signaling the beginning of the Republic of Texas. Yet the conflict between Texas and Mexico would continue for the next 10 years.

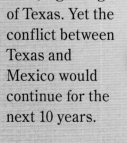

Battle of San Jacinto
In Gary Zaboly's painting *Onward was the Cry!* five soldiers surge toward the Mexican army's breastworks: a Tejano, a Texian officer, a U.S. Army deserter, a Kentucky flagbearer, and a backwoodsman. The flagbearer carries the Liberty Flag of Colonel Sidney Sherman's volunteers, topped with a lady's white glove.

Original Bowie Knife
James Bowie, a co-commander at the Alamo and leader in the Texas Revolution, was renowned for his knife-fighting exploits. This knife, created by his brother Rezin, is part of the Alamo collection.

Antonio López de Santa Anna

A controversial figure in Mexican politics, Antonio López de Santa Anna Pérez de Lebrón was born in 1794. He served in the Spanish Royalist army, but in March 1821, he switched allegiance and fought for Mexican independence. Santa Anna rose to power in Mexico City and was elected president as a Federalist in 1833. The following year, he joined the Centralists. Santa Anna led the charge against the rebels in the Texas Revolution, taking no prisoners at the Alamo. He was captured at San Jacinto, however, and forced to recognize Texas. After the war, he was briefly exiled before returning in 1846 to defend his country in its war with the United States. Santa Anna then suffered a lengthy exile. In 1874, he returned to Mexico, penniless and unknown. He died in Mexico City in 1876.

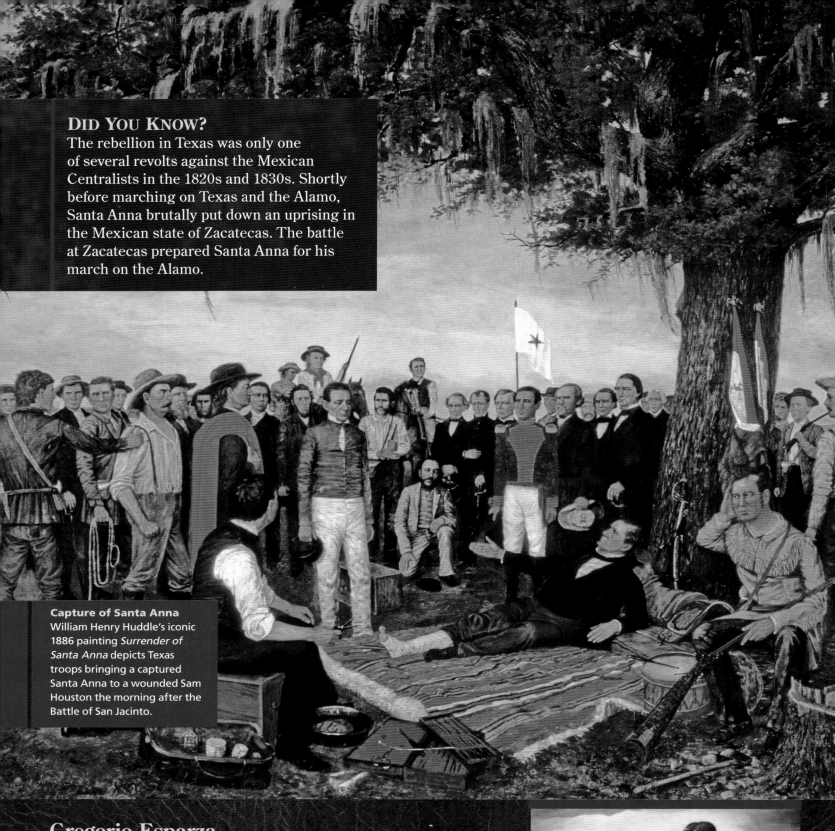

DID YOU KNOW?
The rebellion in Texas was only one of several revolts against the Mexican Centralists in the 1820s and 1830s. Shortly before marching on Texas and the Alamo, Santa Anna brutally put down an uprising in the Mexican state of Zacatecas. The battle at Zacatecas prepared Santa Anna for his march on the Alamo.

Capture of Santa Anna
William Henry Huddle's iconic 1886 painting *Surrender of Santa Anna* depicts Texas troops bringing a captured Santa Anna to a wounded Sam Houston the morning after the Battle of San Jacinto.

Gregorio Esparza

José María Esparza, better known as Gregorio Esparza, was born in 1802 in San Antonio de Béxar. Esparza enlisted in Juan N. Seguín's company in October 1835 and participated in the Siege of Béxar. When Santa Anna arrived in February 1836, Esparza and his family took refuge in the Alamo. Lieutenant Colonel William Barret Travis later allowed local citizens to leave the Alamo, but Esparza elected to stay and fight. His family remained with him. He died in the Battle of the Alamo on March 6, 1836. After the siege, Gregorio's brothers received permission to enter the Alamo and search for his body. They took the body and interred it in the Campo Santo on the west side of San Pedro Creek.

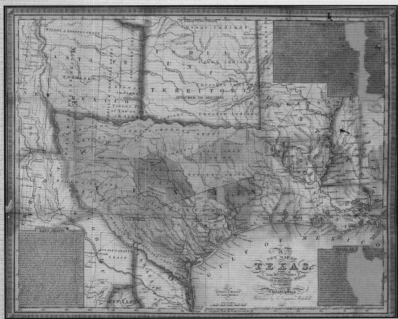

Sketch of the Alamo
This 1844 sketch depicts the Alamo as it sat abandoned for years after the battle— a source of limestone for builders and a curiosity for visitors.

Santa Anna's Medallion
Santa Anna gave this religious medallion, made in 1805, to one of his captors after the Battle of San Jacinto. It is engraved with the figure of Nuestra Senõra de Guadalupe, the patron saint of Mexico.

Map of Texas
This 1836 map depicts Mexican Texas with its color-coded *empresario* colonies, Nueces River southern boundary, and the lack of any Panhandle settlement.

"The cause of Philanthropy, of humanity, of Liberty & human happiness throughout the world call loudly on every man who can, to aid Texas.... If we succeed, the country is ours, it is immense in extent and fertile . . . and will amply reward all our toils. If we fail [,] death in the cause of liberty and humanity is not cause for shuddering."

—Daniel Cloud, Alamo defender, December 26, 1835

Control of the Cannon
Gary Zaboly's scene *The Fight for the Eighteen-Pounder* shows the soldiers fighting for control of the Alamo's largest cannon after it was turned to fire at the Mexican soldiers in the compound.

James Bowie

James Bowie was a soldier, slave trader, land speculator, explorer, and the South's most formidable knife fighter. Born in Kentucky in 1796, Bowie became internationally famous for his knife skills after the Sandbar Fight of 1827. He arrived in San Antonio in 1830, gaining more fame when he took an expedition to find the legendary Los Almagres Mine (the "lost" San Saba Mine) and fought off an Indian war party. During the revolution, Bowie led troops in the Battle of Concepción and the Grass Fight. At the Alamo, he shared command with William B. Travis. On February 24, Bowie fell ill and was confined to a cot. Tradition holds that Bowie emptied his pistols on the attacking Mexican soldiers before he died, cementing his status as a Texas hero.

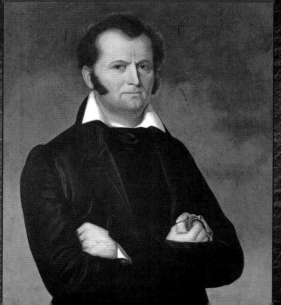

The Siege of the Alamo

February 23 - March 6, 1836

The arrival of General Antonio López de Santa Anna's army outside San Antonio on February 23, 1836, nearly caught the rebels by surprise. Undaunted, they withdrew across the San Antonio River and prepared to defend the Alamo. Among them were lawyers, doctors, farmers, and a former congressman and famous frontiersman from Tennessee named David (Davy) Crockett. Most of the men were in their 20s and most were Anglo, but there were a handful of native Tejano defenders as well. Legendary knife fighter and land speculator James Bowie shared command with lawyer and former schoolteacher William B. Travis.

As soon as the siege started, Travis sent out pleas for help. On the eighth day, 32 volunteers from Gonzales arrived, increasing the number of defenders to nearly 200. The final assault came before dawn on March 6, 1836, as columns of Mexican soldiers attacked the Alamo's walls from all sides. Travis was one of the first defenders killed as he stood atop the North Wall. Bowie was most likely killed on his sickbed. Many believe Crockett survived the initial attack but was put to death by Mexican soldiers soon afterward.

The struggle continued for 90 minutes until the defenders were overwhelmed. By sunrise, the battle had ended and Santa Anna had entered the Alamo compound to survey the scene of his victory.

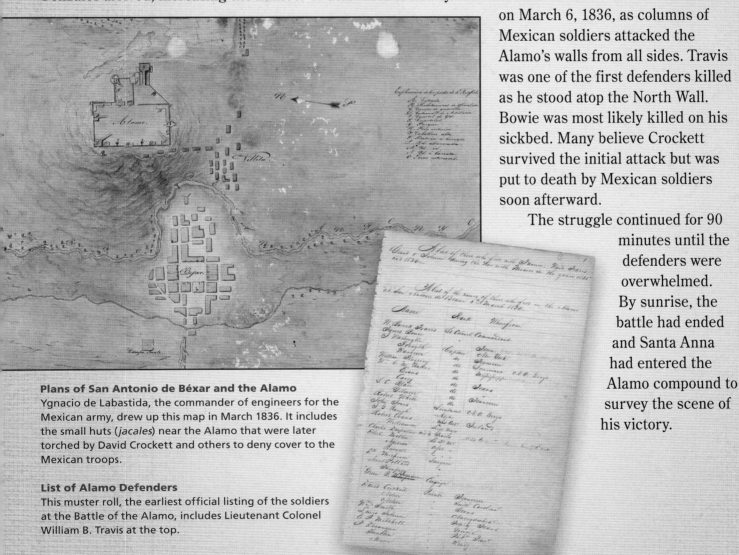

Plans of San Antonio de Béxar and the Alamo
Ygnacio de Labastida, the commander of engineers for the Mexican army, drew up this map in March 1836. It includes the small huts (*jacales*) near the Alamo that were later torched by David Crockett and others to deny cover to the Mexican troops.

List of Alamo Defenders
This muster roll, the earliest official listing of the soldiers at the Battle of the Alamo, includes Lieutenant Colonel William B. Travis at the top.

"Much blood has been shed, but the battle is over; it was but a small affair."

—General Antonio López de Santa Anna to aide Fernando Urriza

DID YOU KNOW?

The flag most often depicted flying over the Alamo—a Mexican tricolor flag with the date "1824"—may not have been there at all. The only flag known for certain to fly over the Alamo was the flag of the New Orleans Greys, which was captured and sent to the Mexican government by Santa Anna as proof that Americans were fighting on behalf of Texas.

Aerial View of the Alamo
Gary Zaboly's *The Siege* shows the Mexican army infiltrating the walls of the Alamo just after daybreak. An *acequia*, or waterway, runs around and through the fortress.

Flag of the New Orleans Greys
This flag, inscribed "First Company of Texan Volunteers from New Orleans," flew over the Alamo during the siege. Santa Anna sent it to Mexico immediately after the battle as proof that "foreigners" were helping the Texians. It remains in Mexico City under tight security.

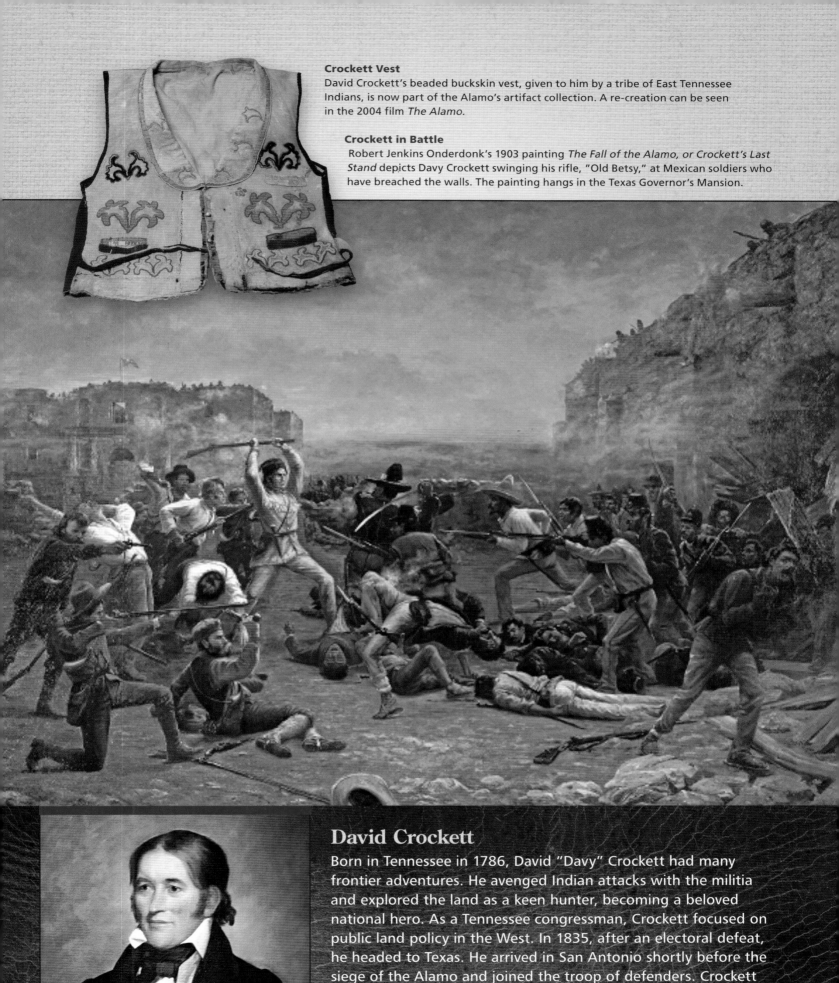

Crockett Vest

David Crockett's beaded buckskin vest, given to him by a tribe of East Tennessee Indians, is now part of the Alamo's artifact collection. A re-creation can be seen in the 2004 film *The Alamo*.

Crockett in Battle

Robert Jenkins Onderdonk's 1903 painting *The Fall of the Alamo, or Crockett's Last Stand* depicts Davy Crockett swinging his rifle, "Old Betsy," at Mexican soldiers who have breached the walls. The painting hangs in the Texas Governor's Mansion.

David Crockett

Born in Tennessee in 1786, David "Davy" Crockett had many frontier adventures. He avenged Indian attacks with the militia and explored the land as a keen hunter, becoming a beloved national hero. As a Tennessee congressman, Crockett focused on public land policy in the West. In 1835, after an electoral defeat, he headed to Texas. He arrived in San Antonio shortly before the siege of the Alamo and joined the troop of defenders. Crockett died after the final assault on March 6. Questions about his death remain, but one eyewitness account stated he was captured alive and put to death by the order of Santa Anna.

DID YOU KNOW?

The weather was not, as many believe, the coldest on record. Several accounts reveal typical Texas weather around the time of the siege—in the 30s, rising to the 60s, and then dropping again after a cold front. According to the writings of Texas citizen William Fairfax Gray, it was "fine weather."

Morning Siege

Henry Arthur McArdle's famous 1905 painting *Dawn at the Alamo* captures the chaotic scene as the Alamo defenders are overwhelmed by Mexican troops. Travis is the dominant figure standing on the wall at right.

Three-Legged Willie

Robert McAlpin Williamson, a lawyer, politician, and friend of William B. Travis, was known as "Three-Legged Willie." Williamson's leg was bent back by polio, forcing him to use a supporting wooden leg. During the siege, he sent a letter to Travis, telling him that reinforcements were on the way. The promised help never arrived.

News of the Battle

Word of the Alamo siege was carried across Texas and the nation in newspapers like this March 1836 edition of the *Telegraph and Texas Register*.

"The enemy in large force are in sight. We want men and provisions. Send them to us. We have 150 men and are determined to defend the Alamo to the last."

—William B. Travis to Andrew Ponton and the citizens of Gonzales, February 23, 1836

Letter from Daniel Cloud
This letter is from Alamo defender Daniel Cloud to his brother, written near Natchitoches, Louisiana, on December 26, 1835. Cloud enlisted in the Volunteer Auxiliary Corps of Texas on January 14, 1836, in Nacogdoches and traveled to the Alamo with David Crockett and several others in a unit called the Tennessee Mounted Volunteers in honor of Crockett, a Tennesseean.

The Aftermath
Because he considered them pirates, Mexican general Santa Anna ordered the bodies of the Alamo defenders be burned immediately to deny them a Christian burial. The exact location of the two pyres remains unknown. This evocative depiction, *Funeral Pyre*, was painted by artist Jose Arpa.

The Travis Letters

February 24 - March 3, 1836

During the nearly two weeks that the Alamo was under siege, Santa Anna encircled the compound, gradually isolating the old fortified mission. Inside, Alamo commander William Barret Travis began writing desperate pleas for help.

As Travis sent out his letters, his couriers slipped past the Mexican lines—sometimes in the dark of night. The first six letters were sent to public officials in nearby towns. They described the dire situation and called for immediate help. The last two, addressed to personal friends, discussed his likely death. By far the best known is the "Victory or Death" letter penned on February 24, 1836, and addressed "To the People of Texas and All Americans in the World." It is one of the most stirring letters in American history and has become an icon of courage under fire.

The nearby town of Gonzales was able to respond to Travis's call for help by sending 32 men from the Gonzales Ranging Company. They arrived early on March 1, 1836. Other troops prepared to send reinforcements, but distance and terrain made it impossible for them to reach the Alamo in time. On March 11, 1836, General Sam Houston arrived at Gonzales to find nearly 350 men assembled and ready to march to the Alamo's aid. Shortly after Houston's arrival, however, word reached the community that the Alamo had already fallen.

The volunteers that gathered at Gonzales became the nucleus of the army that Houston took to San Jacinto. There, the cry "Remember the Alamo!" spurred Texians to defeat Santa Anna and his troops in only 18 minutes.

Line in the Sand
In his piece *Moment of Decision*, Gary Zaboly depicts William B. Travis drawing his legendary line in the sand to rally his troops in the plaza. An ill James Bowie reclines on a cot near the front.

The Travis Ring
Near the end of the siege, Travis gave this agate "cat's eye" ring to 15-month-old Angelina Dickinson, knowing she would likely be spared.

"If this call is neglected, I am determined to sustain myself as long as possible & die like a soldier who never forgets what is due to his own honor & that of his country—Victory or Death!!!"

—William B. Travis, February 24, 1836

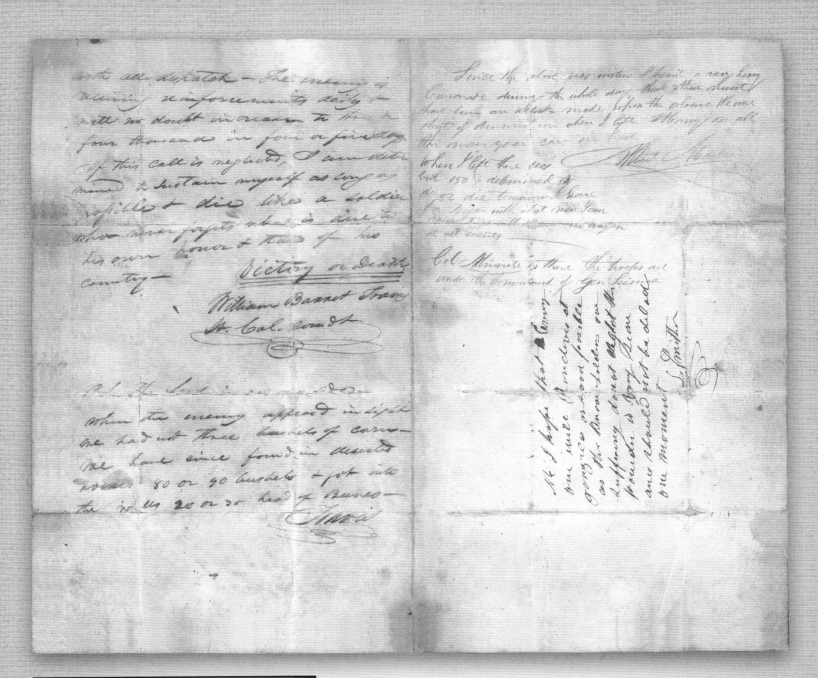

"I shall have to fight the enemy on his own terms, yet I am ready to do it, and if my countrymen do not rally to my relief, I am determined to perish in the defense of this place, and my bones shall reproach my country for her neglect."

—William B. Travis to Jesse Grimes, March 3, 1836

Travis's Son

Charles Travis, seen here as a young adult, was only seven years old when his father died at the Alamo. William B. Travis's last letter from the Alamo asked his friend David Ayers to "Take care of my little boy." Charles later served in the military but died at an early age.

Copyrighted 1900

Anson Jones

Anson Jones was a doctor, congressman, and the last president of the Republic of Texas. As a congressman, he helped regulate medical practice in the republic, advocated a uniform system of education, and championed an endowment for a university. Jones also became minister to the United States and secretary of state. Dubbed the "Architect of Annexation," he worked with President Sam Houston on two fronts, hoping to achieve the goal of annexation by the United States or independence from Mexico. Jones was elected president of Texas in 1844 but soon became unpopular, censured by the Texas congress and scorned by citizens. After his term ended, he became a prosperous planter. In 1849, Jones suffered a debilitating injury and became increasingly morose about his public rejection. He committed suicide in 1858.

Under the Republic

1836 - 1845

After two sieges and a bloody battle, many buildings in the Alamo compound were damaged, burnt, or pockmarked by heavy cannonade. Before he marched east in pursuit of Houston's army, Antonio López de Santa Anna assigned Colonel Juan José Andrade and his troops the task of occupying and repairing the Alamo. The Mexican army maintained control of San Antonio until May 1836. That month, the soldiers received orders to demolish the Alamo before they withdrew. They knocked down some of the outer walls of the compound, including the log wall known as Crockett's Palisade, to prevent it from being easily refortified by the Texians.

The period of the Republic of Texas was difficult for San Antonio and the Alamo. Sam Houston's victory over Santa Anna did not end the fighting. Mexico refused to give up its claim to the republic. Cross-border invasions—or "expeditions"—inflamed hostilities. Both nations lacked the resources necessary to hand the other a decisive defeat. With San Antonio located on a war-torn frontier, the Alamo remained unoccupied. Republic of Texas troops abandoned and reoccupied the old mission several times. Often, they pillaged the Alamo for souvenirs, carving up parts of the wall and the religious statues left from the mission era.

Despite being war-weary and nearly bankrupt, Texas was still a coveted prize for annexation. To stave off British involvement in Texas, the U.S. Congress authorized a resolution to join Texas to the United States. Texas became the country's 28th state in 1845. On February 19, 1846, Texas accepted the agreement in a ceremony. Anson Jones, the last president of Texas, declared, "The final act in this great drama is now performed. The Republic of Texas is no more."

First Photograph
This 1849 daguerreotype of the church is the oldest photograph taken in Texas and the only known image of the Alamo before it was repaired and rebuilt by the U.S. Army in 1850.

Approval of Annexation
On July 4, 1845, Texas delegates authorized the annexation of Texas to the United States. Pictured is the first page of the *Journal of the Annexation Convention.*

End of the Republic

Anson Jones, president of the Republic of Texas, lowers the Republic of Texas flag on February 19, 1846, while stating, "The final act in this great drama is now performed. The Republic of Texas is no more."

Texas Map

This 1849 Texas map illustrates the state's claims to lands from the present-day states of New Mexico, Oklahoma, Colorado, and Wyoming. These claims were settled in the Compromise of 1850.

Alamo Drawing

Texas pioneer and diarist Mary Ann Adams Maverick, wife of Samuel Maverick, sketched the Alamo in 1838. Her memoirs and illustrations provide a vivid record of life on the Texas frontier. After the battle, the Mavericks lived next to the Alamo and helped develop the surrounding area.

"Companions in Arms!! These remains which we have the honor of carrying on our shoulders are those of the valiant heroes who died in the Alamo. Yes, my friends, they preferred to die a thousand times rather than submit themselves to the tyrant's yoke."

—Juan Seguín at the burial of the Alamo defenders' ashes, 1837

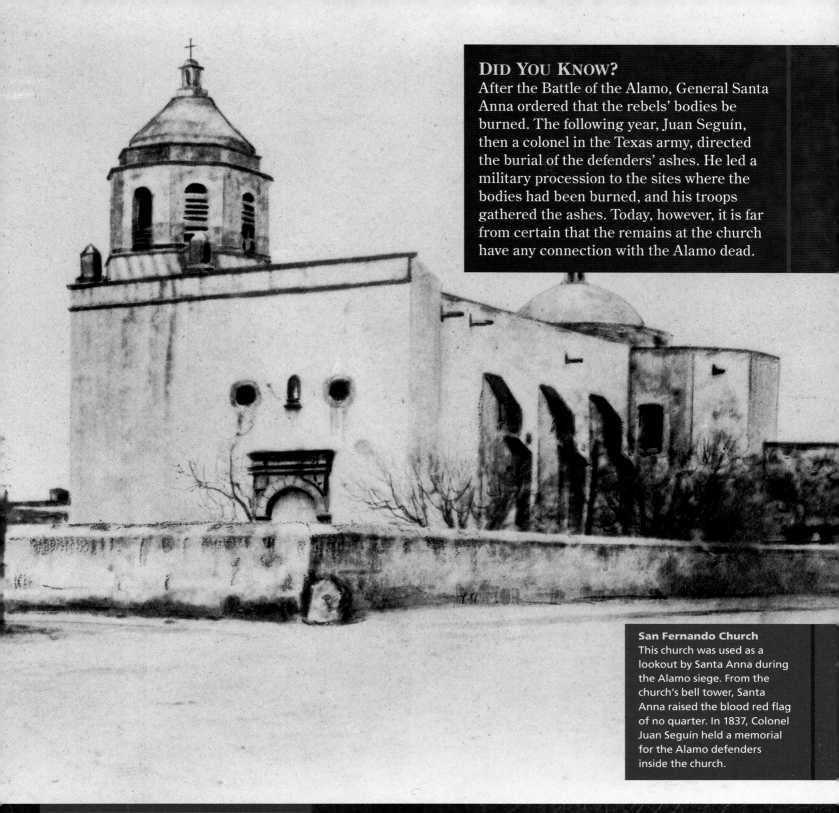

DID YOU KNOW?
After the Battle of the Alamo, General Santa Anna ordered that the rebels' bodies be burned. The following year, Juan Seguín, then a colonel in the Texas army, directed the burial of the defenders' ashes. He led a military procession to the sites where the bodies had been burned, and his troops gathered the ashes. Today, however, it is far from certain that the remains at the church have any connection with the Alamo dead.

San Fernando Church
This church was used as a lookout by Santa Anna during the Alamo siege. From the church's bell tower, Santa Anna raised the blood red flag of no quarter. In 1837, Colonel Juan Seguín held a memorial for the Alamo defenders inside the church.

Sam Houston

Sam Houston was born in Virginia in 1793. As a boy, he ran away to live with the Cherokees and was later wounded in the War of 1812. He then moved to Tennessee and was elected congressman and governor. After a failed marriage and a period of self-exile in Indian Territory, he relocated to Mexican Texas. There, he joined the Texian rebels. Houston signed the Texas Declaration of Independence and was named major general of the army. Failing to relieve the Alamo, his troops defeated the Mexican army at San Jacinto. Houston was elected president of the republic and served in the Texas congress. After annexation, he became a U.S. senator and governor of Texas. In 1861, he was removed from office after refusing to swear allegiance to the Confederacy. He died in 1863.

The Army Moves In

1846 - 1877

★

Once Texas joined the Union, all its forts were transferred to the U.S. Army. Centrally located and vital to Texas, San Antonio remained an important civic and military asset. Thus, the U.S. Army decided to make the Alamo a regional quartermaster depot to supply the forts guarding the expansive Texas frontier.

The army made many renovations and converted the old convent building into a warehouse. By 1850, it had expanded its work to the church, filling up the old colonial arches to create doors, adding windows, and building a pitched wooden roof, the first ever for the old building. Engineers faced a problem, however, in elevating the front of the church to cover the roof. Their solution was to add an arched parapet to the front—giving the Alamo its famous rounded "hump."

The army's presence brought security back to San Antonio, and the town flourished as a military and commercial hub. During this period, Samuel Maverick developed the area around the Alamo into a planned community called "Alamo City." Yet the Alamo would change military hands again. During the Civil War, Texas voted to join the Confederate States of America, and in February 1861, U.S. troops surrendered the Alamo to Confederate forces without a shot. The fortress would remain in Confederate hands until the U.S. Army returned after the end of the war.

By 1876, the army needed larger facilities. The U.S. Army relocated to the new Fort Sam Houston to the north and in 1877 left the Alamo for the last time.

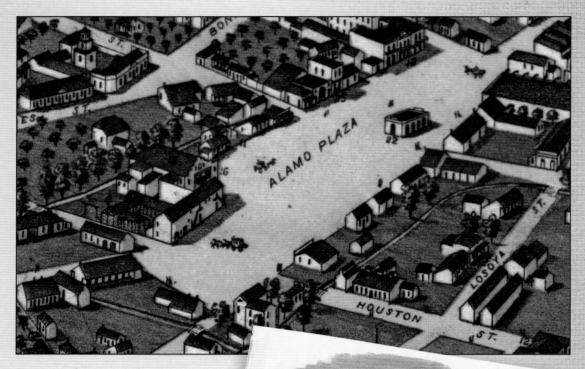

San Antonio Perspective Map
This 1873 map detail provides a bird's eye view of the Alamo and its surrounding area during the years the U.S. Army occupied the fortress.

Civil War Surrender
This *Harper's Weekly* painting depicts Texas secessionists seizing the Alamo from U.S. general David E. Twiggs on February 16, 1861. Twiggs agreed to surrender all federal property and evacuate the 2,700 Union troops scattered throughout the state.

Did You Know?

Although the U.S. Army believed annexation gave it the right to the Alamo property, the grounds and buildings were still owned by the Catholic diocese of Texas. After a short legal battle between the army and the Catholic Church, the court ordered the Quartermaster Department to pay rent to the diocese for the use of its property.

Samuel Maverick

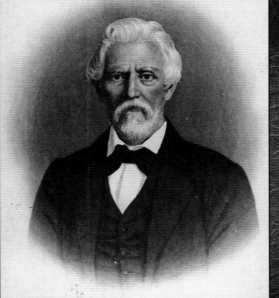

Samuel Augustus Maverick arrived in San Antonio in 1836, shortly before the Siege of Béxar. He was put under house arrest by Mexican general Cos and kept a vivid record of the siege. Upon his release, Maverick guided Benjamin Milam's division to attack. Maverick also fought at the Alamo, leaving the siege on March 2 to sign the Texas Declaration of Independence. After the revolution, he served as mayor and treasurer of San Antonio. He was later elected to the Congress of the Republic of Texas and advocated for annexation to the United States. A wealthy land baron, Maverick was known for his unbranded cattle. His wandering herd gave rise to the term "maverick," meaning independently minded.

Plaza and Cannon
A lone cannon is seen in this 1861 image of the open plaza. A similar cannon, seen below, is on display at the Alamo.

Alamo in Ruins
Soldier and artist Edward Everett sketched this 1847 image of the Alamo, bottom, just three years before the army added the rounded "hump" and upper windows to the façade.

DID YOU KNOW?

During the Mexican War (1846-48), nearly 3,000 American soldiers passed through San Antonio on their way to Mexico. One of them, Edward Everett, was a volunteer from Illinois who stayed in Texas after being wounded on guard duty. A draftsman, Everett found work with the U.S. Quartermaster Department, becoming the chief clerk at the Alamo depot. His work documenting the appearance of the Alamo prior to 1850 appeared in several government reports and publications.

Drawn by Edwᵈ Everett   C.B.Graham lithog

RUINS OF THE CHURCH OF THE ALAMO, SAN ANTONIO DE BEXAR.
Scale 10 feet to an Inch

San Antonio Development
Hermann Lungkwitz's 1857 oil painting *Crockett Street Looking West* is one of the earliest views of the back of the Alamo (shown on the far right).

Colt Revolver
The 1860 Colt Army .44 caliber revolver, likely worn by U.S. Army troops stationed at the Alamo, was the most widely used revolver of the Civil War.

Alamo Upper Story
An 1892 photograph shows the wooden roof and upper story of the church, which was added by the U.S. Army when the Alamo served as a warehouse. The second story was removed in July 1895, and the wooden roof was replaced by a concrete roof in 1921.

"The Alamo, on the left bank of the river, if placed in a suitable state of repair, would accommodate a regiment, and might at the same time be rendered a strong defensive work, well supplied with water."

— George W. Hughes, Captain, Corps of Topographical Engineers, Chief of the Topographical Staff, U.S. Army, 1846

Adina De Zavala and Clara Driscoll

Adina De Zavala, right, was the granddaughter of the first vice president of the Republic of Texas and a teacher, historian, and preservationist. In 1903, she led the efforts to save the Alamo's Long Barrack, or *convento*. De Zavala met Clara Driscoll while fundraising at the Menger Hotel. Driscoll—a wealthy philanthropist whose grandfathers both fought in the Texas Revolution—agreed to supply the money. Yet the women soon disagreed on which buildings were most important to the Alamo legacy. In 1911, De Zavala provided documentation to save the Long Barrack, which Driscoll wanted to demolish to improve the view of the iconic church. Eventually, the Long Barrack was partially demolished, and with time, only the church and its famous "hump" became identifiable with the name "Alamo."

Warehouse to Shrine

1877 - 1905

The Alamo compound was divided and sold when the U.S. Army departed in 1877. The Catholic Church claimed ownership of the remaining mission buildings, while the city maintained ownership of the roads in front of the old church. That year, French businessman Honore Grenet purchased the Long Barrack, or *convento*, where he operated a museum and general store. Grenet added a wooden porch, balcony, and fake cannon turrets to the building. He also rented the church as a warehouse and painted his name across the curved parapet. When Grenet died in 1883, the Long Barrack was sold to a wholesale grocer, Hugo & Schmeltzer Company.

The state purchased part of the site after Sam Houston's son Temple, a state senator, authored a bill directing the state to purchase the church from the Catholic diocese for $20,000. The transfer took place in May 1883, and the City of San Antonio hired a custodian for the site.

In 1903, Gustav Schmeltzer decided to sell the Long Barrack to make way for a new hotel. Preservationist Adina De Zavala started a public campaign to save the historic building. She partnered with Clara Driscoll, who advanced the money to buy the Long Barrack for $75,000 on behalf of the Daughters of the Republic of Texas (DRT). Two years later, the Texas Legislature appropriated the money to reimburse Driscoll and the DRT. The bill—sponsored by President Lyndon Baines Johnson's father, Sam Ealy Johnson—entrusted the Alamo to the DRT as a custodian to maintain it as a shrine to Texas liberty.

Alamo Chili Stands
This circa 1905 postcard shows the early commercialization of Alamo Plaza in front of the Long Barrack. The large brick building is the post office.

Clara Driscoll
Driscoll worked with Adina De Zavala and the Daughters of the Republic of Texas to acquire and preserve the Alamo. As the financier, Driscoll gained national publicity as the "Savior of the Alamo."

1905 Texas Law
This law provided for the state's purchase of the former Hugo & Schmeltzer building and its care and preservation as a historic site by the Daughters of the Republic of Texas.

President Roosevelt speaking to an immense crowd on front of Historic Aalamo, San Antonio, Texas.

Political Rally at the Alamo
In this postcard dated 1904, President Theodore Roosevelt speaks at the Alamo. Numerous billboards stand atop the former Long Barrack.

Save the Alamo
This postcard, dated 1907, captures a colorful float in the Battle of Flowers Parade. The parade began in 1891 to honor the heroes of the Alamo and the later victory at San Jacinto.

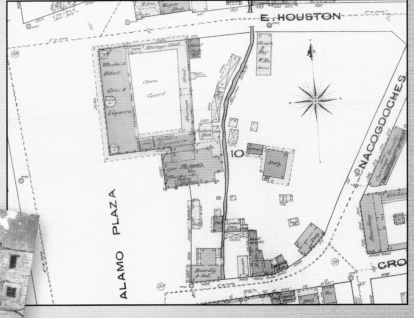

San Antonio Sanborn Fire Insurance Map
This July 1885 map of the Alamo and surrounding area during the warehouse period shows the wooden buildings in yellow and stone buildings in blue. Insurers used these maps to determine fire risks. Liquor was stored adjacent to the Alamo church.

"No monument that could be erected by the hands of man could be as great or sacred as the Alamo itself."

—Adina De Zavala, San Antonio preservationist, 1936

DID YOU KNOW?
No one is certain what is carved on the keystone above the entrance to the church. One historian states that the carving bears the date "1758" and the monogram "Ave Maria." Another believes the monogram is composed of the letters "M.A.R." for "Maria Angelorum Regina" (Mary Queen of Angels).

Church Keystone
A 1961 detail of the keystone above the church entrance shows the intricate carving created by Spanish craftsmen in the 1750s.

Flag Song of Texas
While fighting to save the Alamo in 1903, the Daughters of the Republic of Texas also held a competition to choose a flag song for Texas.

FLAG SONG OF TEXAS

DEDICATED TO
HON. WILLIAM L. PRATHER, LL.D.
PRESIDENT OF THE UNIVERSITY OF TEXAS,
BY THE DAUGHTERS OF THE REPUBLIC
OF TEXAS

PRIZE SONG.

WORDS BY
LEE C. HARBY

MUSIC BY
ALDRIDGE B. KIDD.

COPYRIGHTED 1903
BY THE DAUGHTERS OF THE REPUBLIC OF TEXAS.
HOUSTON, TEXAS.

General Merchandise
For 20 years, the Long Barrack functioned as a general store and grocery operated by Hugo & Schmeltzer Company.

The Modern Era

After custodianship of the Alamo passed to the Daughters of the Republic of Texas in 1905, the organization was fractured by competing visions as to how to best preserve the site. The state took brief custody of the Alamo in 1912 and began restoring the site. Custody was restored to the DRT that year, and in 1913, the upper-story walls were removed from the Long Barrack, or *convento*. As the centennial of the battle approached in 1936, the compound was renovated into a park-like setting as a memorial to those who died. When Driscoll passed away in 1945 and De Zavala in 1955, their bodies both lay in state in the Alamo church.

The Alamo was designated a National Historic Landmark in 1960 and listed in the National Register of Historic Places in 1966. In 1968, the Daughters of the Republic of Texas opened a museum in the Long Barrack, putting the oldest building on the Alamo grounds back into use.

In 2011, the Texas Legislature granted authority over the Alamo to the Texas General Land Office (GLO). The GLO signed an agreement to keep the DRT in charge of the Alamo's daily operation. It also created a private nonprofit group, The Alamo Endowment, to assist with large-scale fundraising. In 2013, the Alamo saw the return of a Texas treasure— the "Victory or Death" letter penned by William B. Travis in 1836. Through a joint project of the GLO, the Alamo, and the Texas State Library and Archives Commission, the original letter was returned to the Alamo for a temporary exhibit. More than 24,000 people viewed the letter during its 13 days on display.

Rare Texas Snowstorm
Snow blankets the Alamo grounds in this 1949 photograph.

Postcard View
A colorized postcard from 1912 shows the park-like development in Alamo Plaza and the ruins of the Long Barrack after the warehouse period.

The Alamo   Restored 1912.
Built in 1718.

"Davy" Crockett

Alamo defender and Tennessee congressman David "Davy" Crockett was larger than life. Even before he came to Texas in 1836, Crockett's backwoodsman alter ego "Davy" was cemented in popular culture as the subject of various books, plays, and songs. After his death, Crockett was portrayed in the movies many times. The earliest was a short fictional film in 1909 called *Davy Crockett—In Hearts United*. A more historically accurate Crockett was portrayed by Cullen Landis in the 1926 film *Davy Crockett at the Fall of the Alamo*. Perhaps the best known and most loved film versions of the backwoods congressman, however, were portrayed by John Wayne in his 1960 epic *The Alamo* and Fess Parker in the Walt Disney film and TV series of the 1950s.

it's MOVIE TIME in TEXAS U.S.A.

JOHN WAYNE

John Wayne
John Wayne, at the time the biggest movie star in the world, makes an appearance at the Alamo in 1951, where he reveals his plans to make an epic film of the Alamo story.

John Wayne's Crockett Cap
John Wayne wore this replica coonskin cap as Davy Crockett in his 1960 movie *The Alamo.* The cap was donated to the Alamo collection.

Peter Ustinov
Actor Peter Ustinov, as Mexican general Maximilian Rodriguez de Santos, rides a white horse in front of the Alamo during the filming of the 1969 movie *Viva Max!*

"Perhaps nothing symbolizes the struggle between freedom and tyranny more than the Alamo. Here, Anglos and Tejanos joined together to fight for Texas freedom. They made the ultimate sacrifice and died so that freedom might live in Texas. Thanks to them, the dream of a free Texas became a reality that endures today."

—George P. Bush, Commissioner, Texas General Land Office

Aerial View
A 1940 photograph shows the grounds of the Alamo. The complex was extensively renovated for the Texas Centennial in 1936.

Postage Stamp
This nine-cent Alamo stamp, created by the U.S. Postal Service in 1956, was part of a series called the Liberty Issue.

Long Barrack Ruins
In 1912, the wooden building erected on top of the Alamo ruins by businessman Honore Grenet was stripped away to remove the non-original parts of the Long Barrack. Only the walls were left standing.

Alamo Research Center
The Alamo Research Center, right, built in 1950, contains the Daughters of the Republic of Texas Library.

Arcade
The stone arches, or arcade, below, were built in the 1930s and lead from Crockett Street (on the Menger Hotel side) to the south side of the church.

Gift Shop
The Alamo Gift Shop, bottom, was originally constructed in 1937 as a museum dedicated to the Texas Centennial.

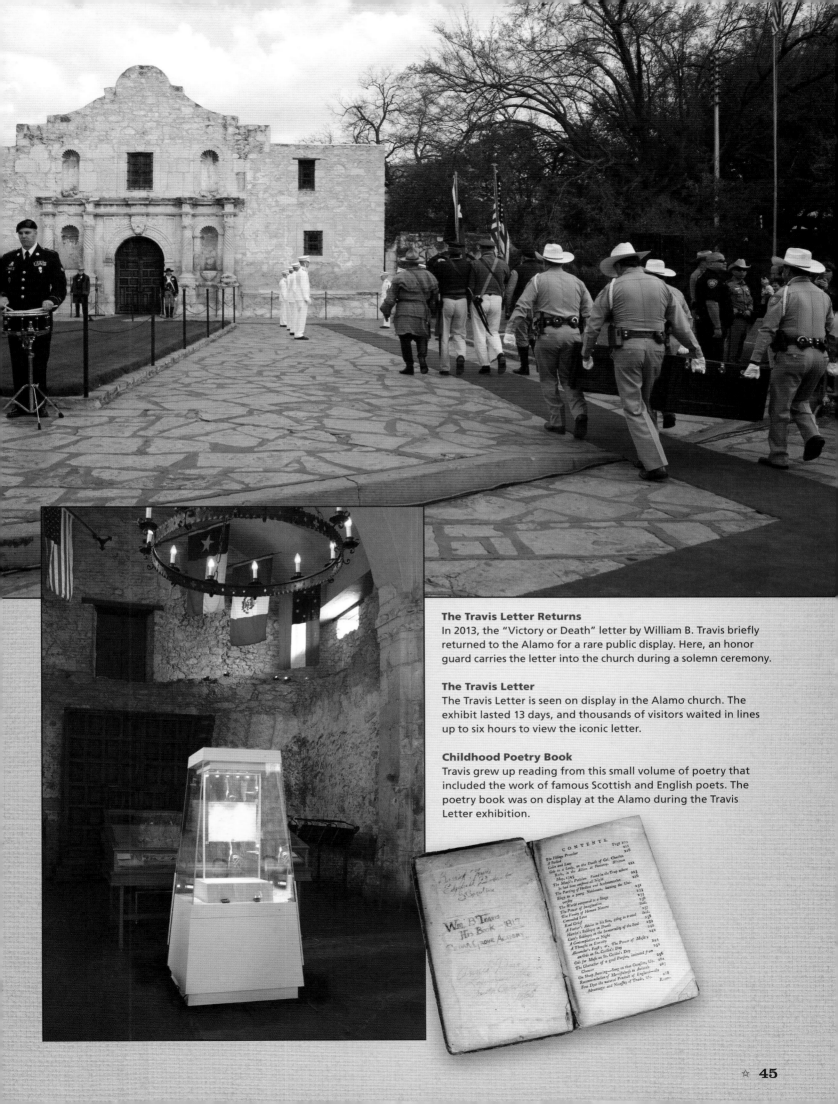

The Travis Letter Returns

In 2013, the "Victory or Death" letter by William B. Travis briefly returned to the Alamo for a rare public display. Here, an honor guard carries the letter into the church during a solemn ceremony.

The Travis Letter

The Travis Letter is seen on display in the Alamo church. The exhibit lasted 13 days, and thousands of visitors waited in lines up to six hours to view the iconic letter.

Childhood Poetry Book

Travis grew up reading from this small volume of poetry that included the work of famous Scottish and English poets. The poetry book was on display at the Alamo during the Travis Letter exhibition.

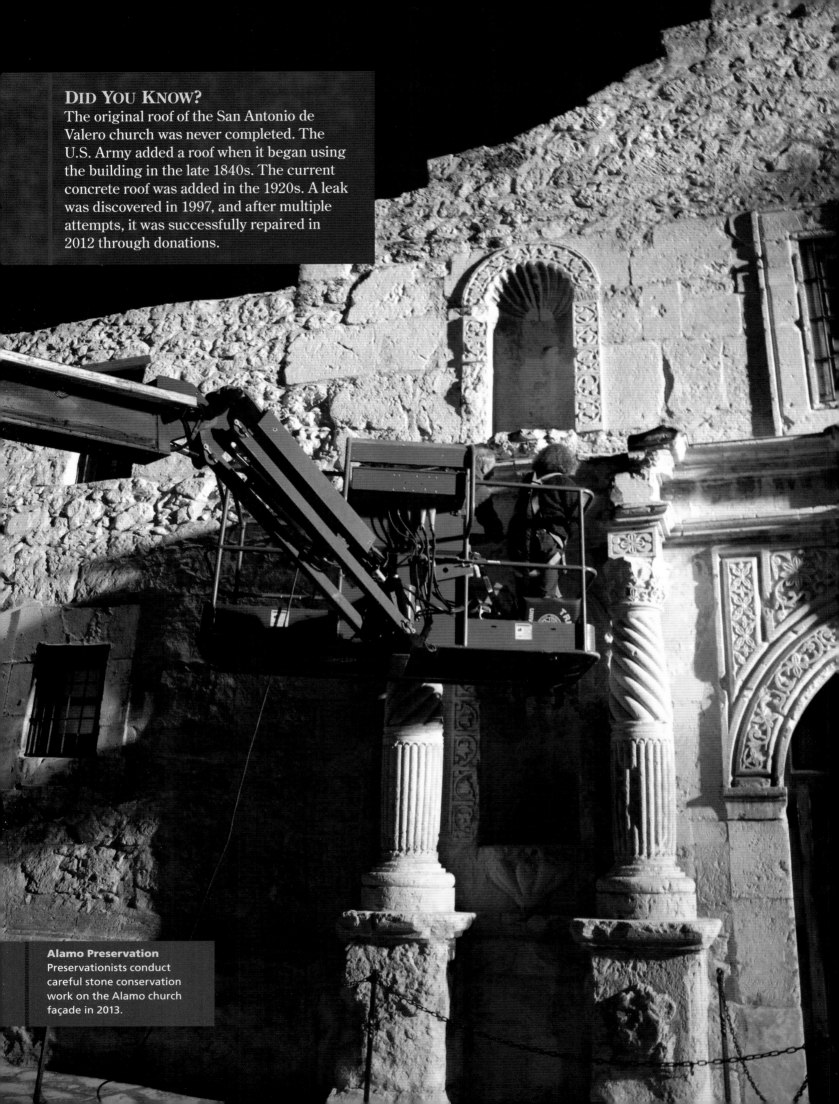

DID YOU KNOW?
The original roof of the San Antonio de Valero church was never completed. The U.S. Army added a roof when it began using the building in the late 1840s. The current concrete roof was added in the 1920s. A leak was discovered in 1997, and after multiple attempts, it was successfully repaired in 2012 through donations.

Alamo Preservation
Preservationists conduct careful stone conservation work on the Alamo church façade in 2013.

Preserving the Past

For 300 years, the Alamo has been at the crossroads of history. From its beginnings as a Spanish mission, to the iconic site of the 1836 battle that enshrined it in the hearts of Texans, to its role in the commercial development of San Antonio, the Alamo is a place like no other.

Its story is intertwined with many others, including the colonization effort by Spain in the New World, the assimilation of indigenous tribes, Manifest Destiny and the expansion of the American Southwest, and the fight between tyranny and liberty. The Alamo is a place that tells us so much about ourselves. It is a place worth saving.

More than 175 years after the historic 13-day siege and bloody battle, the Alamo remains under attack. Today, the complex is threatened by slow decay due to the passage of time and a public that views the Alamo as a picturesque backdrop instead of a pioneering Spanish mission and shrine to honored dead.

Located in the center of a thriving downtown, the Alamo—the state's top tourist attraction—is also threatened by commercialism and loss of historical integrity.

Preservation efforts at the Alamo are ongoing and expensive. From uncovering the many layers of plaster inside the church to protecting the fragile and iconic façade, the goal is to preserve the Alamo for future generations. The remarkable story of the Alamo—all 300 years of it— must be passed on to ensure the meaning of the place is preserved along with the buildings. With proper attention and care, future generations will always be able to remember the Alamo.

Thermal Imaging
A preservationist uses a special camera to take thermal images of the Alamo façade. Thermal imaging helps study the effects of temperature and moisture on the delicate stonework.

Spanish Mural
This detail of a Spanish colonial era mural with a floral and pomegranate pattern was discovered by Mary C. Jary and Alamo conservator Pamela J. Rosser.

Created by Texas Land Commissioner Jerry Patterson in 2004, the Texas General Land Office Save Texas History program is a statewide initiative to rally public support and private funding for the preservation and promotion of historic maps and documents that tell the story of Texas.

With the twin goals of preservation and education, Save Texas History seeks to conserve these documents for future generations while educating Texans about the rich heritage found in these vital records.

Unfortunately, many of these documents are crumbling into dust due to age, overuse, and previous poor storage conditions. Yet no general revenue from the Texas Legislature is appropriated for this purpose. The conservation and promotion of these Texas treasures depends solely on private donations, map purchases, and corporate sponsorships.

www.savetexashistory.org
www.thealamo.org

The historians and staff of the Texas General Land Office and the Alamo contributed to this book in the spirit of saving Texas history for future generations.

Texas General Land Office:
Mark Lambert, Mark Dallas Loeffler
The Alamo: Bruce Winders

Photo Credits:
Images are identified from top to bottom and left to right:
Alamo Collection: 2–3, 5b, 7a, 7b, 8b, 9a, 9b, 13a, 14b, 16b, 17b, 18a, 20a, 21a, 23b, 24a, 24b, 25a, 25b, 31b, 34b, 35c, 42b, 45c; Fotografia tomada en el Archivo General de la Nación: 12b; Briscoe Center for American History, the University of Texas at Austin: 19a, 29a, 30a, 40b; Cushing Library Archives of Texas A&M: 34c; Daughters of the Republic of Texas Library Collection, Alamo Research Center: 4a, 22c, 23a, 28a, 32b, 33b, 34a, 35b; Driscoll Foundation: 37c; Friends of the Texas Governor's Mansion: 21b; Library of Congress, Prints & Photographs Division: 13b, 31a, 38b, 39a; Courtesy of Daniel Mayer: 11a; Museo Nacional de Historia, Mexico City: 20b; National Portrait Gallery: 21c; Public Domain: title page, 7c, 22b, 30b, 38a, 38c, 39c, 41b, 43c; Vito Alessio Robles, *Coahuila y Texas*, 1946, v. 2, frontispiece: 10b; Texas Beyond History, College of Liberal Arts, the University of Texas at Austin: 4b; Texas General Land Office: front cover, 5a, 11b, 14a, 17a, 17c, 19b, 26b, 30c, 32a, 37b, 39b, 41a, 44a, 44b, 44c, 45a, 45b, 46, 47a, 47b; *Texas Highways* Magazine: 36b; Texas State Library and Archives Commission: 10a, 26a, 27a, 27b, 29b; Texas State Preservation Board: 13c, 15a, 16a, 18b, 22a, 28b; San Jacinto Museum of History: 15b; University of Texas at San Antonio Libraries Special Collections: 6, 8a, 33a, 36a, 37a, 40a, 42a, 42c, 43a, 43b; Witte Museum: 35a

The Alamo: 300 Years of Texas History was developed by Beckon Books in cooperation with the Texas General Land Office and Event Network. Beckon develops and publishes custom books for leading cultural attractions, corporations, and nonprofit organizations. Beckon Books is an imprint of Southwestern Publishing Group, Inc., 2451 Atrium Way, Nashville, TN 37214. Southwestern Publishing Group, Inc., is a wholly owned subsidiary of Southwestern, Inc., Nashville, TN.

Christopher G. Capen, *President, Beckon Books*
Betsy Holt, *Development Director*
Monika Stout, *Senior Art Director*
Kristin Connelly, *Managing Editor*
Jennifer Benson, *Proofreader*
www.beckonbooks.com | 877-311-0155

Event Network is the retail partner of the Alamo and is proud to support its mission of education, history, and preservation. www.eventnetwork.com

ISBN: 978-1-935442-38-7
Printed in the United States of America
10 9 8 7 6 5 4 3 2